Spirit Party

—

Why Give It
How to Give It
What to Give

Anita Forrester

Speed Light Books
New York

Copyright © 2011

All rights reserved. No part of this book may be used or reproduced or translated without the written permission of the publisher.

Published by:

Speed Light Books
P.O. Box 458, New York, NY 10159, U.S.A

ISBN: 978-0-9832579-0-5

CONTENTS

INTRODUCTION 7

WHAT IS A SPIRIT PARTY 11

WHY GIVE IT.. 13

    SPECIFIC REQUEST FROM SPIRITS 13
    TO ASK FOR HELP, GUIDANCE OR OTHER FAVORS 13
    IF YOU ARE A TORMENTED WORSHIPER 14
    DIFFICULTY IN COMMUNICATING WITH THE SPIRITS ... 14
    FAMILY HERITAGE 15
    ASK FOR FORGIVENESS 16
    THANK THE SPIRITS 17
    PROTECTION AND SAVING YOUR LIFE 17
    GOOD LUCK AND GOOD OPPORTUNITIES 19
    REMOVING CURSES, SPELLS AND HEXES 19
    PUNISHING PEOPLE WHO CAUSED YOU UNHAPPINESS. 19

HOW TO GIVE A SPIRIT PARTY 21

    PREPARE YOURSELF.. 21
    ABOUT WOMEN AND THEIR MONTHLY CYCLE 22
    SET THE TABLE... 23
    COOK THE FOOD.. 27
    THE PARTY.. 29
    WORSHIP WITH A SPOUSE OR PARTNER 31
    WHAT SHOULD BE DONE WHILE THE PARTY IS GOING ON 33
    AFTER THE SPIRIT PARTY 34

- THE SPIRIT BATH 34
  - WHAT IS A SPIRIT BATH 34
  - WHY TAKE A SPIRIT BATH 35
  - IF YOU DON'T TAKE A SPIRIT BATH 35
  - HOW TO TAKE A SPIRIT BATH 36

WHAT TO GIVE 39
- STANDARD SPIRIT PARTY 39
  - TRAVELING SPIRITS 42
  - FORGIVENESS PARTY 42
  - FAMILY HERITAGE PARTY 45
  - THANK YOU PARTY 45
  - ASK SPIRITS FOR SPECIFIC HELP 46
  - WEALTH 47
  - ATTRACT GOOD LUCK, REMOVE BAD LUCK, HEXES, CURSES 47
  - PHYSICAL AND PSYCHOLOGICAL HEALING, HEALTH 48
  - SUCCESS IN BUSINESS, ATTRACT CLIENTS, INCREASE PRODUCTION 50
  - LOVE PROBLEMS, FINDING A COMPATIBLE PARTNER, STRONG MARRIAGE, CHILD WELFARE 51
  - EVERYTHING JOB RELATED: GET A JOB, JOB PROMOTION, JOB SECURITY, TROUBLE WITH CO-WORKERS 52
  - SPECIAL DRINK 52
  - PLANTAIN PUDDING 53
  - SPECIAL PUDDING 54

SOME FINAL THINGS YOU NEED TO KNOW 57

INTRODUCTION

Spirits are all around us. People all over the world, from different cultural backgrounds, recognize their existence. In Africa and Asia people worship the spirits of their ancestors. People of European descent pray to angels and saints. Buddhists keep miniature temples for gods in their homes. Hindus love their gods and goddesses.

All of these people connect to the spirits they believe in by the offering of food. For example, Africans give their ancestors food and libations. In Mexico, and other Latin American countries, the Day of the Dead is celebrated by placing elaborate meals on graves. The dead spirits are called forth to enjoy the food. In Ireland, during the Samhain festival, food is left outdoors for spirits. There are many other examples that you may know about.

In these pages you will learn how to connect with spirits by giving a spirit party. This information can be used for any kind of spirit, such as ancestral spirits, guardian angels, traveling spirits or others.

Food and beverages are served at a spirit party just as they would be at an ordinary one like a birthday or a graduation party, etc. But there are differences, since spirits are not humans. This book reveals the procedures for preparing and serving the food. Some of these procedures will make sense while others may seem strange as they are designed to conform not to the rules of our world but to those of the spirit world.

You will learn how to know if spirits are helping you; how spirits ask for parties and let you know what they want; and ceremonies and rituals to use before, during and after the party.

You will also learn how to prepare yourself, what foods to buy, how to set the table, what to say and do at the party, and what to do when the party is over.

You will be able to give a spirit party at anytime for certain reasons. Perhaps you need help for a new job, or you have a love problem. You will find the information on what food to serve for your request.

A spirit party can be performed discreetly in your home or with invited guests. What is important is that the proper procedures are followed. You will find in the following chapters all the details to correctly give a spirit party.

Meat and fish, vegetables, bread and sweets are common to most people, but different cultures may use local foods that are not listed in this book. Similarly, some local alcoholic beverages may be different from what is mentioned in these pages. Don't worry if you don't eat all of the foods mentioned in this book. Spirits will want, and accept, foods and alcoholic beverages from the regions where you live. A vegetarian will not be expected to serve meat.

This book gives information about the foods you may not know about and how to prepare them, such as the Special Spirit Stuffing. Recipes are provided for foods and drink mixtures required by spirits when they are asked to fulfill specific requests, such as a petition for good luck.

These pages reveal everything you need to know to give successful spirit parties.

WHAT IS A SPIRIT PARTY

A spirit party is what you give the spirits in return for the help they provide you and your family. By giving the party you are acknowledging to them that you know that they exist and that they are helping, guiding and protecting you. So it is a ceremony in the form of a party to honor spirits, to ask them for favors or to thank them for wishes granted. A spirit party is almost like an ordinary one—food and beverages are served, and sometimes guests are invited. But there are important differences as you will see.

The food and beverages are chosen depending on the purpose of the party. The food is prepared in a specific way and the party table is set according to certain rules. Once these initial preparations are completed, the actual ceremony is conducted in which the spirits are invited to participate.

WHY GIVE IT

In the following pages, we explain some of the major reasons to give a spirit party and describe some special situations when a spirit party may be required.

SPECIFIC REQUEST FROM SPIRITS

Spirits may specifically request that you give them a party. They can do this through a dream or by intuition or other ways revealed only to the worshiper.

TO ASK FOR HELP, GUIDANCE OR OTHER FAVORS

Spirits can help you and guide you in all aspects of your life, whether it be in business, love or other personal matters. If you are seeking help from spirits for a particular purpose, you may give a spirit party and make your request.

IF YOU ARE A TORMENTED WORSHIPER

You may hear voices calling you. You may feel a presence near you. You may feel suffocated in the night or wake up and feel a pressure on your neck or on your chest. You may have recurring nightmares. You may feel something pulling you in a direction that you don't want to go. You may feel and hear disturbing things.

The spirits are not able to talk to you clearly so they create these torments to force you to investigate to find out why you are experiencing them. If this happens you can make a promise to give a party for the spirits. If a spirit party is the answer to your torments, and you give one, you will feel better in a few hours. Otherwise, a spirit party is not the answer.

DIFFICULTY IN COMMUNICATING WITH THE SPIRITS

Sometimes it may seem that no matter how hard you try, you cannot make contact with spirits. Often you have made contact but there is no reason for the spirits to communicate with you. They are not to be called on a whim. They are there for you when there is something really important that you need to know about. When there is something that you need to know they communicate it to you in dreams. Sometimes they can place you in a dreamlike state, as you would be in a daydream, so they can communicate with you. Generally worshipers are

Spirit Party: Why Give It, How to Give It, What to Give

waiting for the spirits to appear in a recognizable form to talk to them. This can and does happen. Sometimes it happens easily, sometimes it doesn't. It depends on the worshiper's natural gift for communication with spirits.

When it is necessary the spirits may communicate with you by forcing you to go in a direction you were not planning to go in; take a job you may not want or leave a job you think you should keep; deal with a situation in a manner that's different from the way you thought to act; or lead you to do something else you normally would not do.

If you really feel that you have not had any communication or if you think the communication is not good enough then you can give a spirit party.

FAMILY HERITAGE

Sometimes a spirit bothers you because someone in your family had been worshiping that spirit in a certain manner. If that person died without telling another family member about the worship and what he or she was doing for the spirit, the spirit will bother someone in the family to get what it wants. The spirit is expecting to be dealt with in the same manner. When it is not worshiped, as it wants to be, it will bother the member of the family that is closest to the one who died. For instance, if your mother or father died, you, as the closest member, will be expected to carry on the worship. Or, it could skip you and pick any member of the family it likes and by whom it wants to be worshiped. If the family member that the spirit settles on doesn't know what to do, he or she will be distressed.

There might have been an ancestor who worshiped a spirit and after many generations the spirit was not able to make its needs known. It may finally find someone in the same family line to settle on for its needs.

If one of these situations applies to you and you do not comply with the spirit's needs you will have little annoying and displeasing things happen to you such as recurring headaches and minor accidents like tripping or cutting your finger or misplacing and losing items.

If you think any of this explanation applies to you and you want to continue to worship the spirit, give a spirit party and ask it to reveal its identity and what it wants so that you may properly serve it.

ASK FOR FORGIVENESS

You may give a party to ask for forgiveness if you make a mistake in your worshiping or if a spirit is punishing you for something you did contrary to spirit rules. The spirits can punish you in various ways such as, causing disturbances in your business and daily affairs, making you intermittently sick, causing you to have headaches and other annoyances such as a stubbed toe.

THANK THE SPIRITS

You can give a spirit party to thank the spirits for everything they have done for you. That is, for the things you know about and the things you don't know about. For example, you thank them for the results you see, such as getting that job promotion you wanted but thought you wouldn't get; and the results you can't see, such as when spirits protect you, save your life, remove hexes and curses from you, and punish people who have caused you unhappiness.

Protection and Saving Your Life

Sometimes it should be obvious when spirits have protected you. For example: You have overslept and missed the plane that was to take you on that long awaited trip. You look at your clock and discover you set it for the wrong time and you berate yourself for being such an idiot for making a mistake like that. Later, you hear that the plane crashed killing all the passengers. In this instance you would be aware of the outcome of what the spirits did for you so you must thank them by giving them a party.

Other times you may not realize that spirits are protecting you. You may feel like walking down a certain street instead of the street where you know your friend is waiting for you. The spirits make you feel this way because they know that danger is waiting for you. Had you taken your intended route you would have been mugged and seriously injured or killed. You would never know that you escaped danger. You would probably be annoyed because you missed your friend. This example shows that you must not think that things will always go the way you want them to or in the way you planned for them to go. When spirits alter your plans or you don't get exactly what you were looking for, it is probably beneficial to you. You can't see all the circumstances and outcomes of your plans but the spirits can. You can give a party to thank the spirits for the protection they gave you, even though you may not know about all the instances when they saved you from harm.

In this final example, you have a plan to grow your business. You do all the necessary planning and hard work. Then you leave everything in the hands of the spirits. They will work for you to succeed whether it takes a shorter or longer period of time than you expected. The spirits know who your enemies are and will thwart their plans to ruin your business or steal clients or contracts. When you are successful in your business, you must give a lavish party to thank the spirits for what they have done for you.

Good Luck and Good Opportunities

You should thank the spirits when they give you luck and provide you with opportunities. Luck may include winning games of chance, or success in love affairs. Usually when you are worshiping spirits you are asking them for something and you must promise to give them something in return. Whenever your goal is accomplished, you give a thank you party. Or if you promised something else, you must keep your promise, whatever it was.

Removing Curses, Spells and Hexes

If you had some curses and hexes or spells on you and the spirits have removed them you must thank them with a party, unless you had promised something else. Whatever you promised to do, you must do.

Punishing People Who Caused You Unhappiness

If you turn a spirit against someone and the spirit has done what it was directed to do, you must thank it because it completed its task and it deserves a reward. You should give a thank you party unless you made another promise to do something else. In that case, you have to keep the promise you made.

Ungratefulness may drive the spirits away from you, and it would be difficult to impossible to get them to return. So, remember to always thank the spirits, even in your daily thoughts.

HOW TO GIVE A SPIRIT PARTY

Since a spirit party is different from an ordinary party that you would give for people, there are many things you must know about and do before you give the party, while the party is going on, and when it is over.

PREPARE YOURSELF

You will begin your day with a shower or bath. You must clean under your fingernails. Before you handle the party food, put your hair under a net or a scarf or other suitable head covering.

If you are suffering from a cold, it is best to wait until you are well before giving the spirit party so that you will not sneeze or cough or blow your nose while handling the food and other party items.

You may have sexual intercourse with your spouse or your steady partner the night before the party. And you may resume your sexual activity after the party has ended, all the party items have been cleared, and the food put away or disposed of.

Plan not to be disturbed. Tell your friends that you will be away the day of the party so that no one will visit or call you. If you are disturbed, don't be frustrated, just deal with the disturbance and resume what you were doing. If you are inviting guests, follow the above instructions. Just schedule the guests to arrive a few hours after the food is presented to the spirits.

About women and their monthly cycle

This is a very important subject for men and women to understand. It is said that when a woman is menstruating she is unclean. In some places, during this time, she is not allowed to handle food or participate in rituals and ceremonies. However, it is ludicrous to believe that because a woman's body is functioning in a normal and healthy way that she is unclean. The spirits know that a woman must menstruate. The Great Architect of the universe made it so. And the Great Architect of the universe didn't make one-half of the world unclean.

The problem is that it is very easy to forget to wash the hands or not wash them thoroughly. When

Spirit Party: Why Give It, How to Give It, What to Give

giving a spirit party everything must be clean. A woman may be in the middle of the food preparation and have the need to change herself and must leave what she is doing to do so. She will have to come back to the food preparation after handling the soiled item. So for reasons of personal hygiene in spirit food handling and preparation, a woman experiencing menstruation should wait until it is over and then give the spirit party.

However, everyday worshiping is okay during menstruation. There is no reason to give up lighting candles and praying. Why should she stop worshiping for seven days (more or less) each month? But we must stress that during this time of the month, a woman must be sure to observe the strictest high standards of personal hygiene as we are sure most women do.

SET THE TABLE

Now that you are clean and, of course, the room in which you are giving the spirit party is clean, the next step is to set the table. You may place all the items on the table in any arrangement that you like. Just make it look inviting and appealing—the way you would want any party table.

Here is a list of the items you will use to set the table for all kinds of spirit parties. You will need:

- Table cloth, white or blue
- Napkins (optional), white or blue
- 3 tall candles, white
- 1 short candle
- 4 candle holders
- Frankincense
- Incense burner
- Matches
- Flowers
- Coffee pot
- Cups and saucers with teaspoons
- Serving platters
- Carving knives, serving forks and spoons
- Plates, dessert plates
- Eating utensils
- Water glasses
- Glasses for alcoholic beverages

You are required to taste all of the food and beverages that you offer to the spirits. So you will need the following items for your personal use:

- A plate
- A dessert plate
- A cup and saucer with teaspoon
- Eating utensils
- A glass for water
- A glass for tasting alcoholic beverages

Set the table with a white tablecloth and white napkins. If your spirit has a color preference you may set the table with it. Otherwise use white. Blue is also acceptable.

Put three white candles in candleholders and place them on the table. The candles will remain unlit until the party begins. Also place some frankincense in a burner on the table. Don't light the incense until the party begins.

Take the short candle and hold it in your left hand and say whatever your wishes are, while twisting the wick with your thumb and forefinger. Then light it and set it in a candleholder and place it on the table. This is the only candle lit so far. Let it burn while you are cooking the food. When the candle burns down, you don't have to replace it. If a portion of the wick remains, even if it is a just a small black piece, save it to use in a spirit bath (see about spirit bath in a later section).

On the party table, put the serving spoons, carving knife and fork, eating utensils, plates and water glasses and other items that you have especially for the spirits. Two of each item should be sufficient. You will need five cups and saucers with five teaspoons because the coffee will be served in different ways as described below.

Place your own set of plates, eating utensils and other items on the table so that you will have them ready to taste the food.

Place the drinks you are going to serve such as wine, rum or gin on the table. Leave the bottles closed but loosen the tops or the corks. Place a bowl of sugar, a cup of honey, a cup of molasses and a cup of milk on the table. You will put a pot of coffee on the table last so that it will be hot.

As each food is cooked, put it in its serving dish and set it on the table. After all the food is set on the table, pour hot coffee into the cups. You must have: a cup with black coffee only, a cup of coffee with milk, a cup of black coffee with sugar, a cup of coffee with milk and sugar, a cup of black coffee with honey, sugar and molasses. So, you will have a total of five cups of coffee on the party table. You will do this for all the spirit parties that you give except for a forgiveness party.

Now you may set the cakes, cookies or whatever dessert you have on the table.

For every spirit party that you give, fill three glasses with fresh water for the spirits. Have a glass of water for yourself in case you become thirsty.

COOK THE FOOD

The most important element in a successful spirit party is cleanliness.

Everything you cook for spirits, everything you serve spirits, everything you touch for spirits must be clean, clean, clean.

This includes the room, floor, table, tablecloth, cooking utensils, dishes, cups, cutlery, glasses, etc. Even dishes on the shelf that you are sure were clean should be rewashed, just in case some dust might have fallen on them.

The meats, vegetables, fish and seafood must be cleaned with lemon juice or white vinegar and rinsed in cold water. Scrub the vegetables with a vegetable brush. These instructions will not be repeated when recipes are given.

Don't do any unnecessary talking and laughing over the food while preparing and serving it so that no spittle from your mouth and no unnecessary amount of your breath lands on the food.

You should keep some food in reserve in case of an accident. For example, if a hair falls into the food, you can replace the spoiled food because simply removing the hair is not acceptable. Imagine seeing someone stick a finger in your pudding to remove a hair.

How would you like to be served some food and find foreign matter in it or notice dirt under your host's or hostess' fingernails or see smudges on the glasses? You would certainly not be pleased with the party or the party-giver.

Just before cooking the food, rub your hands with a piece of lemon then rinse them. When you taste the food for proper seasoning — the food should be flavorful — either clean the spoon after each taste, or have several spoons for tasting.

Never season spirit food with dried or fresh hot peppers unless a spirit asks for it.

If while you are cooking the food or carrying it to the party table some of it drops to the floor, don't be upset. It is usually a good sign that the spirits are pleased with what you are doing. Leave it on the floor.

If no food drops don't become anxious waiting for that to happen. It doesn't mean the spirits are displeased. Spirits make things happen only when they are necessary for reasons we will never know.

While you are cooking, talk to the spirits, mentally or aloud. You could say these or similar words:

> "You will like this cake I have for you."
> "This is a tender piece of meat I selected for you."
> "I am happy that you have been protecting me and my family."
> "If you were not helping me I would have missed that good opportunity."
> "I am thankful that you are with me."

Follow your intuition or feelings. If you have a specific request from a spirit, follow it and buy what it asked for. Sometimes you may be directed to a specific store to buy what the spirit requested. If you have no intuition or special requests, don't worry. It simply means that the spirits are pleased with what you are doing.

THE PARTY

The party begins after all the food has been cooked and set on the table.

Now you must take a second bath or shower and put on clean under and outer clothes.

Light some incense and carry it to the four corners of the party room and let the incense smoke rise into the four corners—that is, north, south, east and west. Then place it on the party table. *Of course you will take precautions against accidentally starting a fire.*

Light the candles at the start of the party. Talk to the spirits aloud and say:

> "I am giving you this party."
> "I have delicious food for you." Say the foods offered.
> "I have all kinds of drinks for you." Say the drinks on the table.
> "I have lots of sweet desserts for you." Say all the desserts on the table.
> "I am giving you this party for..." Explain the reason for the party.
> "I have coffee for you and water."

Proudly name each item, point to it and talk about how rich or expensive or succulent or refreshing the item is and how you chose it especially for the spirits. Now you may say whatever your wishes are, that is, what you want the spirits to do for you.

You will leave the party food untouched for at least four hours before you help yourself to the food and drink. You may take large amounts of what you like to eat and only small tastes of what you don't like. *But you must taste everything.* You can just put a little of something you don't like on your

Spirit Party: Why Give It, How to Give It, What to Give

tongue to taste it. For instance, you may not want to drink alcohol so you would simply wet your tongue with some. Of course, you would taste it from your own glass.

Food must be left on the party table for at least five hours. The hours that the party ends should be after midnight. You may also leave everything on the table overnight and remove the food in the morning.

Don't think your party is a failure if you don't see food and drink disappearing before your eyes. Since they are not human, spirits do not eat as we do. At the end of the party, the table will be as full of food as it was at the beginning except for what you have eaten. No one can say for sure what the spirits do with the food. Perhaps they absorb the odor and devour its essence.

The only ways your party could be unsuccessful are if you failed to keep everything clean or if you didn't fulfill a specific request from a spirit.

WORSHIP WITH A SPOUSE OR PARTNER

Worshiping spirits is a private matter. You should not discuss what you are doing with anyone else. If you are fortunate enough to have a spouse or partner who is also a spirit worshiper, everything will be easier. You will not have to hide what you are doing. For example, maybe only one of you has a spirit communication to give a party for a specific reason. You will be free to spend the money for the food, prepare the food, and have the party without the other person being upset or argumentative or just nosey. If you want, your mate can help with shopping and cooking but must leave you alone for the actual party.

The two of you can give spirit parties together. But each of you must be alone to talk to the spirits during the parties. You may have things you want to say that you don't want your mate to hear. So respect each other's privacy.

If your mate is not a spirit worshiper, you will have to be creative in order to give spirit parties. One idea is to combine a birthday or anniversary celebration with a spirit party. When you take a bite of cake or a sip of wine say mentally:

> "I'm enjoying this for you."
> "This is the only way I can worship you at the moment."
> "I ask that you to make it simpler for me to worship you."

Or, before the celebration, load a plate with food and set it aside as if you were saving it for later on. Say these or similar words:

"This is for you. I hope you like it."
"Help my situation to improve so I can give you a better party."
"Thank you for all your help."

Depending on your particular situation, you may come up with other ways to give a spirit party without your mate knowing. What is important is to always tell the spirits mentally or aloud why you had to give the party the way you did.

WHAT SHOULD BE DONE WHILE THE PARTY IS GOING ON

In some parts of the world, such as regions in Africa, Asia, South America, and the Caribbean, a spirit party is not secret because people are accustomed to giving them. Sometimes a spirit party has several guests. And the guests know that they are at a spirit party and they behave the way they are supposed to. When the party is over, the food is distributed to the guests to take home.

You may also invite people to the party without telling them that it is for spirits. The food can be given away if someone asks for something, just as would be done at a regular party.

During the hours that the food is untouched the guests and the host or hostess at a cultural party sing, perform rituals, beat drums and dance. They do this simply to while away the time.

If you are giving a personal party with no guests invited, you may pray, sing, dance, read, nap or just relax while the food remains untouched. If you want to beat drums you may do that also. If a candle burns down, replace it with another one so that there are always lighted candles on the table. Sometimes the spirits may inspire you to do one or all of the things we have mentioned.

If you have guests, just behave as you would at any ordinary party. Invite the guests to arrive a few hours after the food has been presented to the spirits. During those few hours, talk to the spirits, thank them, tell them your wishes and let them know that guests will be arriving to enjoy their party.

AFTER THE SPIRIT PARTY

Leftover food can be wrapped and stored for yourself and your family to eat. The liquids can be used to give yourself a spirit bath (see below). Any food that you don't want can be given away or thrown away. You can drink the alcoholic beverages from time to time if you want to. If you are giving another spirit party you must buy new bottles of alcohol.

THE SPIRIT BATH

What is a spirit bath

A spirit bath is a bath that you take using a mixture of the liquids that were served to the spirits at their party. This special mixture includes the various cups of coffee, alcoholic beverages and the fresh water that was set on the party table for the spirits.

It is best to take the spirit bath at the end of the party, but if for some reason you can't take it right away you may wait for another day. All you have to do is pour the liquids in a jar or a bottle and close it securely. It should not be refrigerated. If you keep it so long that it starts to ferment, you can still use it although it may not smell so good.

Why take a spirit bath

You take a spirit bath to help improve your intuition; make your communication with spirits clearer; make it easier for spirits to communicate with you; make your dreams more vivid; improve your ability to make good decisions about your personal affairs by being more susceptible to spirit guidance; and other benefits that may be communicated by spirits to their worshipers.

If you don't take a spirit bath

You don't have to take a spirit bath. Nothing bad will happen to you if you don't. The spirits are unconcerned whether you take one or not. Simply, you will forfeit the good benefits explained above. You would just throw the liquids away. So, it is your choice whether you want the added benefits or not.

How to take a spirit bath

In a large bowl mix all the liquids that were on the party table as thoroughly as you can. Drop in the wick, or whatever is left of it, that you saved from the short candle. Do not include liquids from your glasses and cups.

If your party included molasses and honey you can add them to the mixture. You don't have to add the entire bottles of whatever alcoholic beverages you had on the table. One cup of each kind of alcohol is enough or if you had one bottle of something pour one and a half cups of it into the mixture. If you had several cups of coffee on the table, pour them all into the mixture. Also the glasses of water that you left for the spirits must be added.

Get into your tub or shower stall. Put something underneath your feet to prevent you from slipping on the mixture.

Just before you take the spirit bath say:

"I'm taking this beneficial spirit bath so that the power of spirits will always be with me to help me, guide me and protect me throughout my whole life."

Pour the contents of the bowl slowly over your head and body. Rub the mixture as evenly as possible over your entire body. Rub it over your face and into your scalp. While you are rubbing the mixture over yourself say:

> "Thank you spirits for coming to my party."
> "Thank you spirits for being with me."
> "Thank you spirits for staying with me."
> "Thank you spirits for not abandoning me and my family."

You may say any other things that you are inspired to say. You can also list your wishes.

Yes, a spirit bath will feel sticky and uncomfortable but you must remember that you are complying with the rules of the spirit world not those of the human world.

After about ten minutes of having the mixture on, you may take a regular bath or shower and wash the mixture off. You may use soap, that is, bathe as you normally would.

If your spouse knows that you worship spirits and wants to join you, he or she may take the spirit bath with you. This is helpful because you can rub the mixture over each other's backs.

WHAT TO GIVE

STANDARD SPIRIT PARTY

You give a standard party when a spirit requests a party but doesn't tell you exactly what you should serve; when you want to ask for help; when you are a tormented worshiper; and when you are having difficulty receiving spirit communication like intuition or clear dreams. Almost all of your parties will be standard spirit parties. At a standard party you should serve an alcoholic beverage and a dish from each category listed:

> Starchy food like rice, potatoes, yams, corn, beans
> Bread
> Desserts, like cake, chocolate
> Eggs
> Alcoholic beverage, such as wine, rum, beer

> Coffee (serve as described in the previous chapter)
> Water
> Fish, seafood
> Meat, such as beef, lamb, pork
> Fowl, such as chicken, turkey, duck, guinea hen
> Vegetables, such as spinach, beets, cabbage

All the foods that you buy will of course come from the country or region in which you live. For instance, in some places you can buy lamb but not pork. In some places, people only eat fish or are vegetarian. The vegetables that you choose will be locally grown.

If you do not or cannot eat some of the foods on this list, serve what you normally eat, that is, what you eat for your daily meal. But always put bread, water, coffee, an alcoholic beverage and a dessert on the party table.

You may receive communication from a spirit or have some intuition or feeling about a food you were not planning to serve. Follow the spirit's request and serve what it wants. Don't disregard this feeling or intuition. If you don't give that food, the party is incomplete.

Spirit Party: Why Give It, How to Give It, What to Give

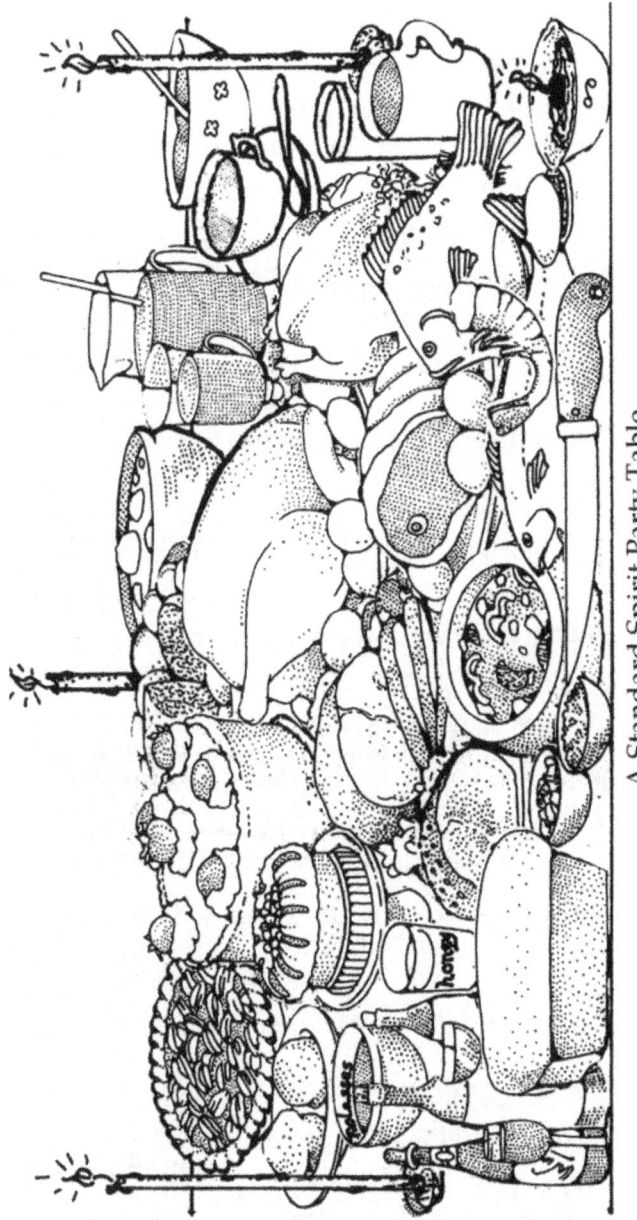

A Standard Spirit Party Table

Traveling Spirits

Traveling spirits are spirits that happen to be passing by. If they like you they will settle with you for a while. When the traveling spirits are with you they can bless you in various ways. Sometimes they heal you and protect you. They often open up opportunities for you. Sometimes you may feel especially good and you don't know why. It could be because one or more of those traveling spirits has befriended you. They don't stay with you. They move on and generally don't return to you.

These spirits partake in any kind of party you give, just like a friend visiting you will eat and drink whatever you have to offer. Since you can't know if a traveling spirit has settled with you, unless they give you a sign, you must remember to specifically acknowledge them and their help at a standard party. You could say:

> "Any traveling spirits that have settled here with me, I invite you to enjoy this party and I thank you for the good things you have done for me."

Or say other words based on your feelings.

FORGIVENESS PARTY

You give this kind of party to ask the spirits for forgiveness. Reasons why you ask for forgiveness are explained in the chapter *Why Give It*. This is a

Spirit Party: Why Give It, How to Give It, What to Give

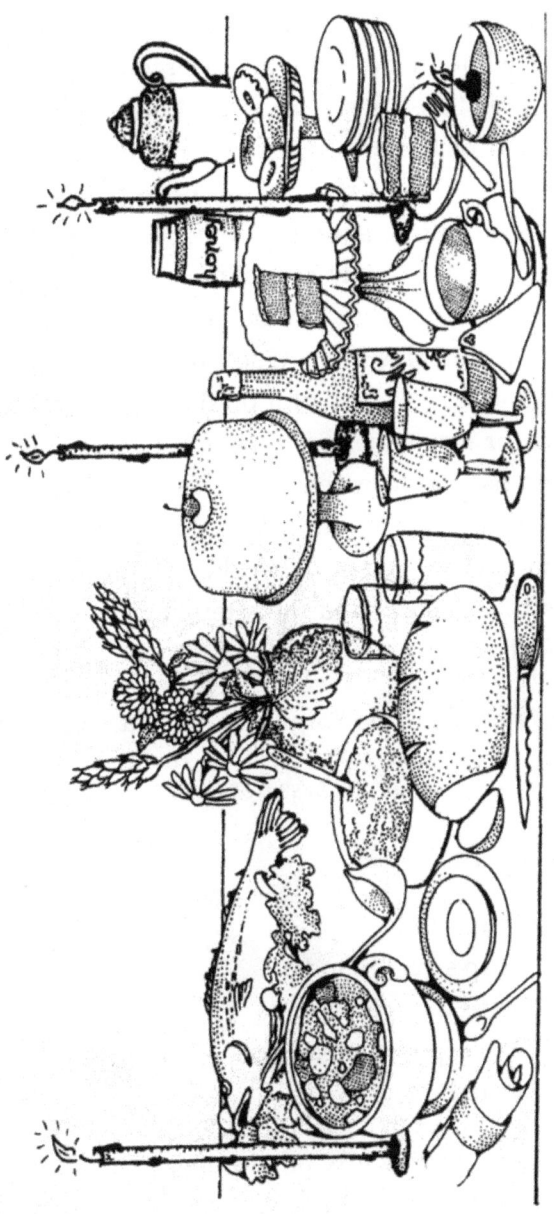

A Thank You Party Table

very small party. You serve desserts, such as cookies or cake, white bread, rum, sweet brandy, a glass of water and the Forgiveness Cocktail (see recipe below). All of these things must be set on a tray. If you don't have one large tray use as many small ones as you need but be sure everything is set on a tray. Set the tray(s) in your bedroom or in your living room. Light one white candle and invoke the spirit and ask for forgiveness. Open the bottle of sweet brandy and throw some of it on the floor three times and ask for forgiveness. Do the same thing with the rum and ask for forgiveness. Throw some water on the floor three times and ask for forgiveness. This party must be given early in the morning between 5:00 and 7:00 A.M. or in the afternoon between 3:00 and 6:00 P.M.

Now make the Forgiveness Cocktail.

Forgiveness Cocktail

You need:

> ½ cup rum
> ½ cup sweet brandy
> 2 cups orange juice
> 2 tablespoons molasses
> ¼ cup honey

In a pitcher mix all the ingredients. Set the cocktail on the tray. Have a glass next to it for the spirit and a glass for yourself. Throw some of the cocktail on the floor three times and ask for forgiveness.

Take small amounts of everything on the tray for yourself to taste. Be sure to taste the cocktail. Leave the food in your room for two hours. Afterwards you can do whatever you want with the food, that is, eat it or throw it away.

FAMILY HERITAGE PARTY

You give a family heritage party if you feel that spirits that used to be worshiped by a member(s) of your family are bothering you. This situation is explained in detail in the chapter *Why Give It*.

Serve the foods you grew up with. That is the foods your grandmother taught your mother how to cook; the foods served for your daily meals and for the family dinners or special occasions. Those kinds of foods would probably have been passed down through generations and the spirits that follow your family would be familiar with them and want to be served those foods.

THANK YOU PARTY

You give a thank you party to acknowledge all the help the spirits have given you. That includes the help you can see and the help you will not know about, like saving you from harm.

This party is like a birthday celebration. You must serve cake, cookies, honey, coffee, a pitcher of milk, and white wine. Place flowers on the party table. You may serve turkey with Special Spirit Stuffing (see recipe below), Chicken Cooked in Milk (see recipe below), a whole baked fish and a whole fried fish. We mean, do not remove the heads or tails of the fish.

ASK SPIRITS FOR SPECIFIC HELP

The recipes given below are to be used when you ask spirits for some specific help. You will choose the dishes that will help strengthen your requests. For instance, if you want good health you would make Chicken Cooked in Milk. Prepare your standard party table, and then place that plate of food on the table.

NOTE: If you are vegetarian, exclude the meat and follow the recipe as closely as you can. For instance, you could make a dish of stuffing using bread and the vegetables that you usually eat. As mentioned before, the spirits do not expect you to serve something that is not a part of your culture.

Wealth

Serve this stuffing when you want to ask spirits for money, expensive clothes, jewelry, cars, expensive furniture, a luxury home.

Special Spirit Stuffing Made with Beef and Pork Livers

You need:

> ¼ pound ground beef liver
> ¼ pound ground pork liver
> Salt
> Garlic
> Onion
> Herbs and seasoning of your choice
> 2 cups bread crumbs

Thoroughly mix the ground beef and ground pork livers with all the seasonings. Cook the mixture over a low flame in a covered pan until done. Taste and add more seasoning, if needed. Then add the bread crumbs and bake the whole mixture for 20 minutes at 375 degrees Fahrenheit.

Serve the stuffing in a bowl.

Attract good luck, remove bad luck, hexes, curses

Serve this stuffing when you want the spirits to give you good luck, remove hexes, curses and bad luck. Do not ask to have any of these bad things put on another person.

Special Spirit Stuffing made with Pork Tongue

You need:

> ¼ pound ground pork tongue
> Salt
> Garlic
> Onion
> Herbs and seasoning of your choice
> 1 cup or more of bread crumbs

Thoroughly mix the ground pork tongue with all the seasonings. Cook the mixture over a low flame in a covered pan until done. Taste and add more seasoning, if needed. Then add the bread crumbs and bake the whole mixture for 20 minutes at 375 degrees Fahrenheit.

Serve the stuffing in a bowl.

Physical and psychological healing, health

Serve the following when you want to ask spirits for health or a healing—whether physical, emotional or psychological—for yourself or loved ones.

Chicken Cooked in Milk

You need:

> 1 chicken, cut up
> Salt

Garlic

Onion

Herbs and seasoning of your choice

3 cups or more of milk

Vegetable oil

Juice of a lemon

Season the chicken. In a large pot add about 4 tablespoons of vegetable oil. Add the chicken pieces. Don't add water. The chicken will cook in its own juices. Add the lemon juice.

Cover the pot and cook the chicken over a medium flame until the juices from the chicken begin to dry. As the chicken browns, add small amounts of milk and stir and turn the pieces so that they will brown all over. If the chicken sticks to the bottom of the pan, lower the flame a little and add more milk. Keep adding milk in small amounts and turning the chicken until it has an even brown color. Now add enough milk to make about two cups of sauce. Cover the chicken and simmer for about 15 minutes. Taste and add more seasoning if necessary. If you want you can thicken the sauce with a little cornstarch. Just add a little water to about two tablespoons of cornstarch and stir it into the sauce.

Success in business, attract clients, increase production

Serve this stew when asking spirits for help solving all business problems. Do not ask to destroy a competitor.

Meat Stew

You need:

> 3 or more different meats (for example, pork, chicken and beef)
> 4 or more different vegetables (for example, string beans, peas and turnips)
> Herbs and seasoning of your choice
> 2 tablespoons molasses

To a pot of water add the meats and vegetables. You can add small amounts of each meat and vegetable so that you have enough to fill a large bowl. Add seasoning. Make it flavorful. Remember not to use the tasting spoon again without washing it. Don't add any hot pepper. Drop in three raw eggs, that is, with the shells on. Add the molasses. You may add a little bit of flour to thicken the liquid.

NOTE: You should eat the three eggs. If you can't eat them all at once, eat one each day for three days. Or if you can't eat eggs for some reason, give them to members of your family. The eggs must not be given to guests.

Love problems, finding a compatible partner, strong marriage, child welfare

Serve this fish stew for all matters of love and for the protection of your children.

Fish Stew

You need:

> Herring or codfish
> A few shrimp
> A few clams and oysters
> A bit of lobster and any other seafood that is available
> 2 tablespoons of molasses
> Herbs and seasoning of your choice

You don't have to add large quantities of any of these things. Add a small bit of whatever vegetables are in season. Add the molasses. Season the fish stew to your taste, with whatever herbs and seasoning you normally use. Add three raw eggs with the shells still on them. Thicken the liquid with a little bit of white flour.

NOTE: You should eat the three eggs. If you can't eat them all at once, eat one and eat the other two the next day. Or if you can't eat eggs for some reason, give them to members of your family. The eggs must not be given to guests.

Everything job related: get a job, job promotion, job security, trouble with co-workers

Serve this soup to spirits and ask them for help with any job problem you may have. Do not ask for someone to be fired or to sabotage another worker.

Special Soup

You need:

> 1 chicken, cut up
> 3 different vegetables
> Herbs and seasoning of your choice
> Hot red pepper (for this recipe only)

Cut chicken into parts and put into a pot of water; add three different kinds of vegetables, for instance peas, green beans, and eggplant, to the pot. You don't have to buy large amounts of vegetables. Just add small bits of each vegetable to the soup. Add the seasoning. *For this soup only, you may add hot red pepper.*

Special Drink

This drink can be served at all spirit parties.

Mélange Drink

You need:

> 2 cups orange juice

¼ cup molasses
2 cups gin

Mix the orange juice, molasses and gin. Pour the drink into three glasses and set them on the party table. Pour a little in a separate glass for yourself to taste.

Plantain Pudding

This pudding can be served as a dessert at any spirit party.

You need:

>1 small green plantain
>1 quart of milk
>½ cup of sugar or sugar to taste
>2 teaspoon cinnamon
>1 teaspoon nutmeg
>2 teaspoon vanilla

When you buy plantain look for green ones that feel firm and are not rubbery when you bend them. Use lemon or white vinegar to scrub the plantain skin with a vegetable brush. Don't peel the skin off, just cut off the two ends. Grate the entire plantain — skin included.

In a large pot mix the grated plantain with a quart of milk. Add the remaining ingredients. Cook over a low flame for about 20 minutes. Stir constantly so that the mixture will not become lumpy. Taste. If needed add more sugar or cinnamon or nutmeg.

This pudding is served warm. You may refrigerate it after the party and heat it the next day or you may eat it cold.

Special Pudding

This is a simple pudding made with white flour. It may be served to spirits as one of the desserts.

Flour Pudding

You Need:

> 1-½ cups of milk
> 1 teaspoon cinnamon
> ½ teaspoon nutmeg
> ¼ teaspoon salt
> 1 teaspoon vanilla
> ½ cup sugar or more to taste
> ¼ cup white flour

Mix the flour with a small amount of water to make a thin paste. Stir the milk and the other ingredients in a saucepan. Heat the mixture over a medium flame and stir constantly as the mixture begins to boil. Continue stirring so that the pudding will not be lumpy. If the pudding is too thin add a very small amount of flour paste. Taste and add more of whatever it needs to make it tasty. Serve flour pudding warm.

SOME FINAL THINGS YOU NEED TO KNOW

Most importantly, don't reveal any communication you may receive from spirits, not even to your partner.

Thank the spirits as often as you can for their help.

Spend only the amount of money that you can afford on a party. The spirits know when you are doing your best.

Don't give a party while you are upset or having an argument. Give a spirit party when you are completely calm and relaxed.

Avoid making frivolous requests. Spirit communication is serious and the spirits will not respond to silliness.

Don't be jealous of what other people have and ask spirits to cause them to lose it. What spirits give you is yours. What the spirits gave another person belongs to him or her. If you try to take from someone else, spirits will cause you to lose what you have.

If you make a mistake while giving the party, don't worry about it. Just continue what you are doing. Avoid making the same mistake next time.

Don't say anything negative about the food you bought or are presenting to the spirits. For instance, don't say "I should have bought a better piece of meat." Be positive about whatever you bought and serve.

Be sincere about what you are doing and you will be sure to give successful spirit parties in the privacy of your home when you are inspired, at any time you have a special request or just to say thank you to spirits who are helping you.

And remember, everything must be clean, clean, clean for spirits.

You have been given valuable information. Use it.

www.ingramcontent.com/pod-product-compliance
Lightning Source LLC
LaVergne TN
LVHW011413080426
835511LV00005B/521